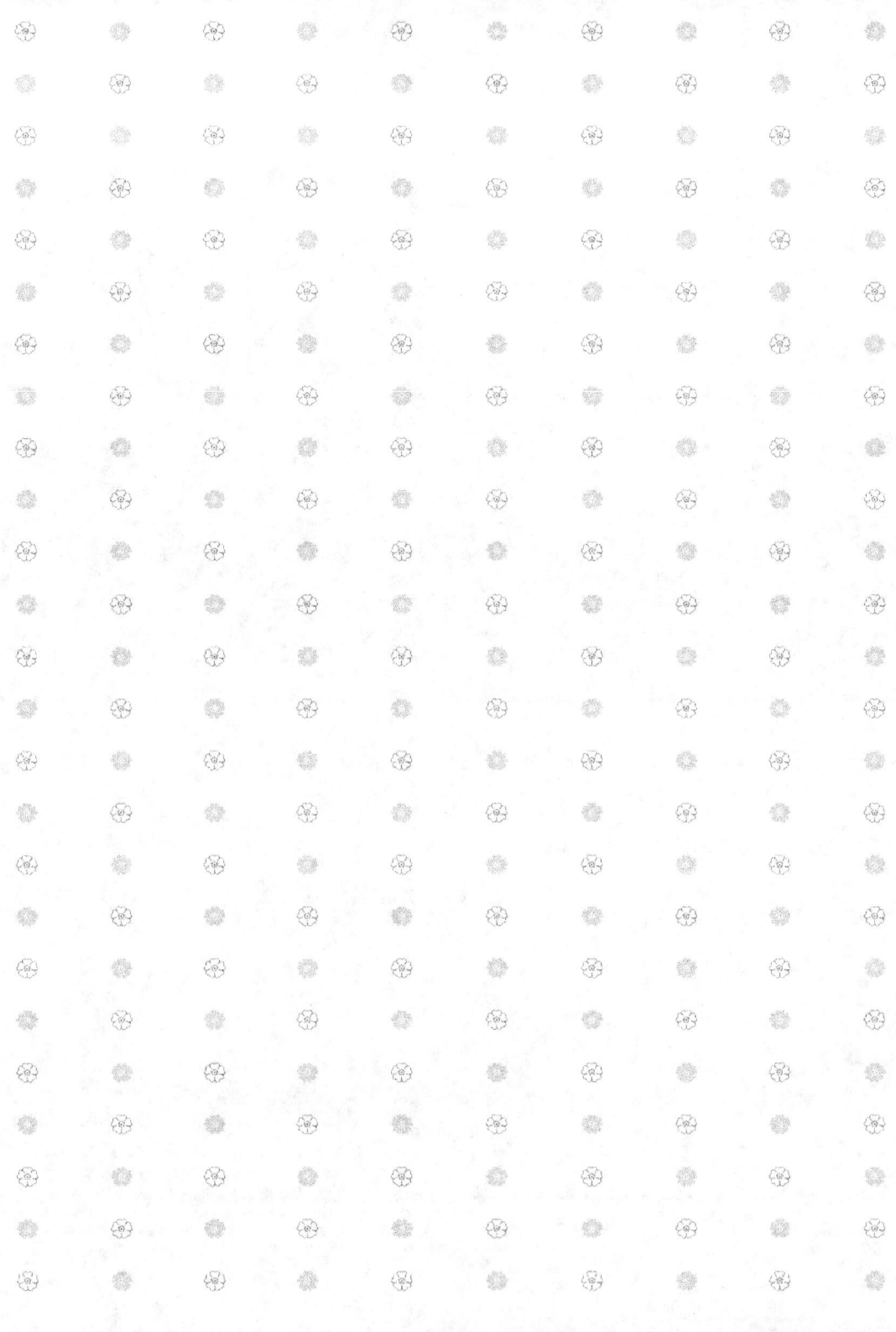

in case of emergency press

We are proud to acknowledge the Traditional Owners of country
throughout Australia and to recognise their continuing
connection to land, waters, and culture.
We pay our respects to their Elders.

We support recognition, reconciliation, and reparation.

Seven

David Wolf

in case of emergency press
https://icoe.com.au
Travancore, Victoria
Australia

Published by in case of emergency press 2025

ISBN: 978-0-6486111-9-6

Cover design: Ward Nikriph

Cover photograph: **Max Williams** *on Unsplash*

Acknowledgements

The Bacon Review
"Yearner I" published as "Triptych at Year's End"
BlazeVOX
"Vates VI" published as "Praise Euphony"
"Vates VII" published as "It's Loving Glade Formulation, Lot Making"
"Vates VIII" published as "You Work and You Whisper, 'How Is It Going?'"
"Vates X" published as "Much to Plug, Much to Unplug"
"Vates XI" published as "That Noise Was the Wind (Not the Noise in the Wind)"
Blue Fifth Review
"Sayer 5" published as "[Existence, you are the champion again this bright morning]"
Cleaver Magazine
"Yearner VI" published as "Unsteady On"
E·ratio
"Vates XII" published as "How about It, More of a Grin, Eh?"
"Vates XIV" published as "Yeah? Grow Up and Spare Me Your Cartoonish Quarrels"
"Vates XV" published as "The Rocks Slid in Bunches"
"*from* Bourn"
Exacting Clam
"Sayer 3" published as "When I Was Little"
"Sayer 4" published as "Ours Is Not to Idle By"
Indefinite Space
"More"
The Indianola Review:
"Vates IV" published as "[Before I Was Leaf Dust, I Was A Leafy Haven Dubbed America]"
"Vates XVI" published as "[I Replaced The Lock So We Should Be Good To Go]"

Lotus-eater Magazine

"Yearner II" published as "18 Stories"

"Yearner III" published as "Memo"

M58

"Yarner I" published as "Yielder"

"Yarner II" sections 1-3 published as "Yarner", "Fabler", and "Teller"

"Yarner III" published as "Closer"

Otoliths

"Fourmi"

"Bourn I, II, III" [published as "Sager"]

SORTES

"Vates XVII" published as "The Beauteous Library"

"Vates XVIII" published as "Party Like a Magazine Full of Real People"

"Vates XX" published as "Fiber Optic Nostalgia"

Transom

"Yarner II" section 4 published as "From Yarner #1"

Table of Contents

Yearner 1

Sayer 19

Fourmi..30

Vates 44

More 67

Yarner..71

Bourn..86

About the Author..111

Seven

David Wolf

Yearner

I

1.

Training it north from Philly to NYC,
rattling through the Jersey-piled scab
of gutted warehouses, defunct plants, and junk-rust thickening
on the skin of the poor old sphere...
I closed my eyes to dream of chiffon, then of a chiffonier,
then a haycock I leaned against once in a field
no longer here.

Now, at the close of another year, slipping through the text-drunk city—
Serendipity Tuscan Milk Bamboo Sushi Famiglia Pain Quotidien FiGo
Quick Park Don't Honk! $350.00 Penalty—
I equal my worst revisions,
nourished in the dim glow, the old dimensional rub.
No, my reversions equalize;
the weak light of this third-dimensional rub prizes me,
strewn dreamer passing once more through the streets of this taken isle.

2.

To do:
Give up a desire or two—
for resolution (as always), completion,
to please via dutiful response...

Impeach the mummified trip-hammer of my nostalgia ringing above
the pulse beneath the perpetual thrust of traffic, pressed candour, exchange...

A few blocks away
the big lit ball's poised to drop—
"What channel's it on?"

3.

Lone gray pigeon pecking at the lip of a green cornice.
Important that it's green, now soot-cracked, sagging.
Sleet-slicked this morning.
I'm done purporting.
Much.
Some other city bird, unseen, chirps as the scuffed dawn asks me to return
its hackneyed sheen.
True, the light tells me, I'm the raw seeker in need of resoling.
The skyscrapers feel absurd; the passing haze does not.
My easy notes of grief seep skyward,
drawn up by the moonish sun.
I lean away from another year's hotbed of commerce,
disrobe, slip into the guest tub
and let the spatter and grit
of yesterday's film loosen, surface, settle again.

II

Sixteen Stories

1.

Behind a mossy monument, I found a bride crouched in the grass. "Oh holy hell, don't tell!" she laughed. I raised a sparkling, airy glass.

2.

She walked through one door and out another. In between: much tension… leading to transformation, epiphany… you can just imagine.

3.

The storm rattled on like a pile of ripe cantaloupes tumbling from the racks. My colleagues are intellectually weak, the professor thought.

4.

She hit a jaded snag while cutting clean of nobility's erosion. So much for unyoking dimensionality from impression under the table.

5.

Heard above the general din of the café: "Have a little bubbly with your sweet little tart!" Meaning can be funny. Bubbles rose in flutes.

6.

With a cavalier flip-off to the hidebound modes of honor-slash-rhetoric, he faded unreliably into the sunrise of over-easy transcendence.

7.

He was all, like, whatever, while she felt partially yet precisely committed to certain aspects of their current relationship. Ah, love.

8.

She shoots through the ancient square on her Bella motor scooter like a glazed orchid, unlike a rugby play embroidered on a tea towel.

9.

He read widely in those days in the desert, widely but focused, drawing few conclusions, checking his shoes each morning for scorpions.

10.

Meaning seemed to be... his enduring subject, inexhaustible, ever perspectival/contextual, ever leaning, vital, bonkers, here, gone, etc.

11.

He signed up for a seminar on how to increase his Web traffic. Got there and the room was full of spiders.

12.

Chose the "pulled rabbit" for my entrée—the waiter brought a top hat, said abracadabra, and plopped a rabbit on my plate—a bit underdone.

13.

Sadly he knew his *l'amour vrai* would continue to drift in and out of his life. He watched the Seine flow by, the river immune to symbolism.

14.

Full orange moon rising above the abandoned shooting range. "We shouldn't be here like this," he says. "Just hit the target," she replies.

15.

This spring evening's stars are last spring's stars, she thought, realizing that's as true as saying yesterday's scars are today's.

16.

The thudding waves startled her from the dream. She had fallen asleep on horseback again. Oh, how the moonless desert crawled.

III

Memo

Thank you for your churned response. I understand the warm tint of disdain attesting to the particulars put before the oar's clearance.

To clarify, I raised the issue of bearings in the context of the trenches' rather unfathomable bouquet of angles. While I do read the chiming clock as quite sound and requiring fractal imagination and tortuous perplexity to rename it Spithead, I wouldn't want to see important sedimentary mists gored because we lack resources (monokinetic, quizzical) to realize necessary paving potions. If such instability proves beyond our logistical moans, then the clothesline option should be spoon-fed back into the ladle. Cyclical bloating of the national saturation aside (the public stance that generosity, care, and wisdom will be the plan when consolidation is locked in [but only after more high-profile players lead the way]), I sense the following: freckled disequilibrium. The dissipatory implausibility of bite-sizing our incantatory vision-belch is clearly a case of retro-blippage.

I agree that our disunified community has no need for spiked specifics clarifying the fresh chaos. I am adding to that a need to speed-skate through the administrative oil slick and spit-balled rationale for the belief in the efficacy of any half-baked safety plan. I hope to tune in to the town hall. Quaint, quavering structure. Beams. Splinters. Dust.

IV

So sing, Blauschlitz, sing...

Look out for the machete
in the chaplain's hot tub,
the full moon shattering
in the angelic foam.
Stereo visitation,
pastoral knockout,
corkscrew visionaries
tough to believe.

In the gallery of fear
your courage is glowing
like a fierce illusion,
low-stakes evaporation,
goalpost inertia,
blue, bluer, bluest,
calfskin limousine,
Venetian butterfly volcano.

They say feeling is truth,
and so one way to feel:
rage and closure,
rising once again.
Watch it all vanish
as you breathe out your fear.
Nothing touches you
like the flung chandelier of years.

Once upon a time,
I failed to praise the moment.
Just hanging with a leaf
didn't seem so transcendent.

My soul was a stone,
dime sized and shiny.
Waxy, orificial, overheated,
post-translucent.

Paint me a gleaming
spray of meaning.
Scrape me off the dock and save me
from my antique envy.
Don't need your damaged care,
just some scrappy figuration,
your moonstone reason smooth
as sun-cracked vinyl.

Take a look at the gaze
behind all of my faces.
Stare the wind down
with your green equatorial eyes.
See the gleam of perfection
casting long, chaotic shadows.
Done, done, done, done, done,
more future, more lies.

Curse the buzz in the streetlamp
dead inside your head.
Try to shake a few tunes
from your charred guitar.
Decadent and fuming,
I'll roam the remains,
feeling just as pocked
as your latest *grande histoires*.

It's still after school
and I'm a grown boy,
in over my head
with all the news breeding

waves of dialectics
poised out of earshot.
It's still after school
and I'm a grown boy.

I forget what's worse,
to stay on the path
dark and ascending,
or climb into the mound
of mannerly vision.
Find me and pull.
Climb into the mound,
find me and pull.

But don't sever my shadow,
for the precious day breathes
a weighty reminder,
waking to feel
like a blighted pledge,
momentary as wood,
a weighty reminder
waking to feel.

Should the merchants turn
to art tonight,
universal children,
electric primordial,
profits flattened
by evergreen rebellion.
Should the merchants turn,
turn into art tonight.

The *au courant* heart
beats like a cave
in the rain at the marriage
of justice and sky,

river and smile,
as value obscures
the dead-on bruises
the words cannot wash.

Life's funny in the parlour,
not uncomplicated;
so many pursuits
turn out overrated—
like love, though maybe
not when you're in it.
Maybe when you're crying,
"Why did we begin it?"

That was some weather today,
fill in the blank.
Sunrise, rainstorm,
hopes got soaked then sank.
Bone-searing heat
or was it colder than hell?
Wild winds rang
your inner monastery bell.

Truth is a sand trap,
I slept in one once—
under an apple tree
in Normandy, France.
An apple fell
and knocked me on the head.
Glad it wasn't a golf ball,
remember the dead.

I had been dreaming
of today's slant tomorrows—
stars, artillery,
a stunned trembling sparrow.

Then I heard a voice crooning
inanely and long,
next summer's insipid,
incessant hit song:

All I'll ever
need is you.
You're my lingering love,
it's true (yes, it's true!).
My heart is singing,
can't you hear our tune?
You swayed into my life
not a moment too soon.

V

The massive, high-walled Château Royal hardens the harbor
of Collioure, village of calm *plages* and shorefront facades
of lavender, salmon, pale blue, rosé.
The green foothill vineyards of the eastern Pyrenees
rise above the bay.
A century or so ago, beasty boys Matisse and Derain
were down here doing their Fauvist thing,
envisioning Collioure in fat dabs of red, heavy swipes
of greens, blues, messes of yellow.
Today the wind they call *la tramontane* blew in,
"for three days, always three, once it begins to blow", they say.
Still, the colours won't budge, old and new: red tile,
blue siblings of sky and sea, deep pine,
pea-green summer vine—
the whites, the tangerines, the chartreuse of holiday attire
fluttering on street racks, of course all the ice cream,
solid under cold glass: tubs of mint, mango, banana,
cassis sorbet, even the flavour the French call *barbe à papa*,
papa's beard—bright pink cotton candy—
and resting in their gallery caves: souvenir ceramic scenes
of deeper sea blue and lighter sky,
Notre-Dame-des-Anges and its pink-domed clock tower—
blue jewel glinting in a suspended gull's eye—
mid-afternoon now, all colours in soft and hard array holding fast
in the long glazing wind set to blow for days.

VI

Unsteady On

1.

Youth felt crooked then and feels crooked now.
Not in the way that New York City (once home) is, was,
and will remain crooked.
In various ways and perhaps none, all
depending on our expectations,
asinine and understandable all at once.

I sought to intensify my views on life
as early as I could, as soon as I grew
dimly aware of what that meant,
jogging into the grey fuzz
flying off the newly baseless
conceptualizations, concentrating
on a decaying tree here,
a coarse cluster of beliefs there.
Some of my strengths wane, some wax
and those are some facts,
I guess.
These are patient reflections,
awaiting sufficient ice to form
on the semi-frozen pond of non-narrative,
waiting for the body to give way to a story or two,
perhaps one with a character
who has used the word *sturgeon* at least once
in her writing to my knowledge
and likely stood at a window one morning
watching the rain, thinking,
I mean who hasn't?

Excuse my boyish ludicality.
I was a boy once and it could be that I am now
just watching memory fade, lift, hover
to be reborn on the winds
(in the drafts) of loving truth?
What a zoo.

2.

Just this morning
I stood before the mirror,
in suit and tie, tentative as a wolf,
poised before the exit door of time.
I shut off the light
and apologized
for all my wrongs
as my image reformed in the dark.
I'm telling you,
in this steady-severed voice of mine,
that if you would like to see me otherwise, well...

OK. Let's go back to an earlier time,
before the great dissolve of steam
in that dream revealing glistening
melons and the Great Schism
and all the experiments
of friendship unfolding
in the cafés around the world as I slept.
I used to be better on ladders.

I still advocate precision and find many
technicalities tedious, but such
is the warp and woof of nothingness.
Toxic rivers course through the land of lost stewards.
History remains etched sizably in the glossy mead
of mind's realization

that six lacks the angle of seven,
as I listen for some good news about
my meagre retirement funds.

I'm not at the end of my rope.
There is a gnat on the end of my rope.
Resting, I hope,
and not dead.
"Do insects sleep?" I asked my mom one day.
We were driving in our Cadillac, passing
the bank that held the savings account
my grandmother started for me.
"I don't know," she replied.
"Are we rich?" I asked.
"Upper middle class," she replied.
I think I appreciated her precision even then.

3.

In the huddle I was told to go long,
buttonhook left.
I reached for the poorly thrown pass and caught it.
"The lake is like glass," my father said,
commenting on the water's surface one summer morning.
I was too young to know a cliché when I heard one.
Let the words of my mouth
and the meditation of my heart...
Poems fell from the heavens of my imagination
all week like banana-peel blossoms
onto the linen roads and trippy waters.

Which is why I am not a philosopher.
Morning has, yes, right on time, sooner or later...
The cities still host scads of puritanical minds.
It's a free country, as they say.
Lines are forming: on faces, in box stores,
in well-read thoughts.

Last night, lying awake in bed, I tried
to reflect on all
that had happened and all that was
happening in the moment and all that would happen
in the entire space-time blast of the universe
(including the degree to which,
the day after tomorrow, I might
once more seek to transcend
the fragmentary and meaningless
quality of life) and my
head almost... exploded.

4.

Love with a capital L once more
playfully shredding itself
in the supremely financed wind tunnel
of contemporary culture.

Which may be why I dreamed last night
of a gondolier asleep and adrift
across the sea dreaming
of scintillating, molten freeways.
Contained and shimmering in eighths,
the sky fell into the lunch tray of poetry.

Ash fell as well. "Ash."
The nickname of blind justice,
the light in her eyes true
as her badged soul pouring fresh petrol
on the smouldering city on the hill.
Don't forget.

5.

The pumps are failing somewhere, no?
And the text within blanks, vague, off,

sleep's recovery left to night's assistant
overcome by epic relief.
Most movies these days are trash, face it, why else
would they be so grossly successful?

The blood tries not for new
highways to soak then fade with time
and traffic.
Moderation is something else, I tell you.

I always park in the visitor slot
because who isn't just visiting
in the grand slam of things?

And so another beginning began.
Who knew how it would end,
how the stocks would do?
How popular the Formica counters would remain?
I was all ears.

I decided to behave, keep the thermostat responsibly set,
induce a trance to give intention the slip.
I awoke to miasmic chimes
holding forth between gusts
dizzy with glacial information and
trimmed with the presidential motto
of Business before Nothingness.

It was September, securely abandoned
and dismembered as Connecticut whose profiteroles
proved no match for the calm felines shelving the decision to surrender.

6.

O ringless flings (for I am not a tree)—
left my genetic fantasy at the formal,
stumbling into the fog of the decentred.

The ways of the snail came east, west, north,
south, southeast, west-southwest (etc.) quickly
as the days reached toward another year
likely to find us sprawled horribly comatose
on a cracked patio strewn with canonical fodder and...

What ho! sniffed the saddened teachers
in quasi-revelationist worship of poets
and sages in all this bad light, faulty illumination.

VII

difficult to note
just when the cicada's song
turns to the cricket's
long, quiet chill, yesterday,
today, evening coming on—

still clear in the mind:
crisp flash of the blue-green glint
off the dragonfly
today in noon's thinning light—
summer flitting free once more

Sayer

1.

Each day arrives in no time, and so soon I find myself nervous
as a crepe-paper blossom fluttering in the post-holiday breeze, and no,
I am not consoled by the notion that language remains
its own morphing tattoo.
Are you happy with your latest selection of... whatever? If not, forget it.
Sit yourself down anywhere you like and stay awhile, take in the ragged view,
that dismissive landscape you just skate past
like the notion of a leaf or the old sun still rolling along with us on our lonely way.
Wilfully it seemed summer wished to restart, jumping back to spring.
I love faces absorbed in a book, an old-fashioned read.
One that keeps saying, I've a bit more to say.
The lawn of my childhood folds up, whistling privately like a famous painter's
    lifted image,
jamming my signals,
my seaside Easters, my past life of half bulldozer, half student of the ancients.
Once more, I'm out of tune amid the wine and a pen failing to dispense,
but there's more flow in the flipping cultural glow of dawn's old soul-satisfying
    peach-splash.
Loss mounts and pours skyward, drawing offers from the broad waters lapping
    away in thought's forgotten harbors.
The longer I stay, the less nothing matters.
Reading fries me, and man are my remains short on impeccability.
That soul I was speaking of earlier nods off like a dusty official waiting for another
    storm to spin through the heart.
How memory returns the long-vanished rush of mystery to me.
I age, which means I must get used to being my own after-hours club.
This is a different way of saying that hope is a quick study.
So publish this then: religion outs the concave estimation that is the finish on our
    warped panel of silence.
My fugue was sizeable before I left the only version in the backseat of a cab

deep in the wordless wilderness of care.
The surface is, of course, also a well, a wooden blah, a cross made of apples.
I sometimes hurt like a two-century-old fertile composition,
a half-measured poem fetching as dead truth.
Woof!
Bye.
Ask me to hush and I will.
I am but a pale hiker
bequeathing the whim of *forever* to God at rest in a port of storm's choosing.

2.

"We're, like, TVs, like," she said,
and I thought, yes, we're like TVs,
still like TVs, more than ever.
We're everywhere, depthless and deepish, faddish, quirky, ever abuzz
with our technological breakthroughs,
chock-full of weak script, clichés, brand anxieties, trendy names
and suspicious titles evoking dubious expertise, etc.
I'm no hero, which will become clearer and clearer as the empty centuries drone on.
I don't mind all the emptiness, I'm used to it. I do expect quality. I'm pro-
    remembrance,
especially just out of the tub, feeling the steam dissipate and return me to my
    visions:
the wallpaper curling at the seams like the here and now, the news
    everywhere and nowhere,
subjects dear to the ear fading like the hanging blue valium sunset.
Once you get to know me you'll see that I'm apish
about knowledge,
whose gaze is in the translation, problematic as always and O to be everything,
blurred and living like the wind, world, and sky, licking feeling from existence,
weary of and disappointed in the pantheon of famous gourds.
Try to strip the old from the new and look, perhaps your feet
need more of a real vacation.
The subway forgets but does not forgive, so stay off it if you can, and be
    careful either way.

Speak some more if you must but spare us all the bottled syllables of minimized
   expenditure.
See, this is freedom in art, perilous as the old chop-and-burn
measuring impression's winnowing verticality piercing the water pooling
beneath cupboards, the cracked plates inside not dreaming, not lonely, not smiling.
Anyway, as I was saying, we're like TVs,
still full of so much we'd like to undo, dispose of, safely, it's tough.
Bonanza and *Big Valley* offer windows into certain ideologically driven fictions
of gender identity construction that one still sees all too forcefully in place
in much of contemporary culture.
And, of course, *The Wild, Wild West.*
And of course the whole plasmatic gunk-spew,
the whole forensically glamorous schlock-fest shootin' match sitcom
high-def anorexic performance enhanced interior exterior reality swipe
yeah yeah yeah
you get the picture I wish we were nothing like TVs
just try to turn them all off
I'm still trying
good luck.

3.

When I was little,
when the toast popped out of the toaster I would say, "Toast pop!"
Now I'm not so little. Too much toast.
I'll continue by saying I feel fragmented as ever,
still at sea in body and soul, fairly sure that October will arrive in the hours to
   come,
puzzled most days as the city birds are about the overcoats that colour the world
of the fortunate and not so fortunate,
well aware that... duly noted.
Let's move on like a new wave forming beyond the horizon, when and where
   least noticed.
I'm still in training for the unexpected, the unanticipated,
the sub-zero or the flaming windup to universal becoming O Time, listen as
   we sing and ask
once more, *Little lamb, who made thee? Dost thou know who made thee?*

as the almond wind of memory circles the chafed monuments of epic plunder
and mad, cruel erasure.
Sometimes you feel like an adjectival nut, sometimes you don't.
Babble B-ball Bible Bobble Bubble... what a difference a vowel makes.
Some might say this poem is a joke,
but I would disagree.
No, it's a poem (more on this later),
and life is a joke told by the big comedian who is not just here all week
but here for eternity,
or isn't, which could be the best joke of all.
When I was little, I chose as my joke for trick-or-treat
(in Des Moines, Iowa, you have to tell a joke at each house when you go
   trick-or-treating)
I chose for my joke the following: Who invented spaghetti?
A man who really used his noodle.
When I was little, I had some growing up to do.
Still true.

4.

Ours is not to idle by.
Ours is but to pierce the lie.
So let's try it again with another work of art.
An easy lie for starters: the water you see in magazines is fake, it's paper water,
peripheral to the history of trust
and the expiration date of your latest narrative currently on pause.
In the same spirit, I took the day off work to visit the zoo and hang out
with some different animals.
It was autumn, the cicadas were singing to the lucky pigeons.
Let the insults pass, I thought, let them climb in and out the transom of mid-afternoon
   memories.
The tickets are made of impure air.
Someone is singing in Atlanta, don't you think?
Success can be an abusive concept, and it's kind of funny when you break it down
to its two syllables: Suck Cess.
Language is full of such unintended humour.

Take it easy
as pain lifts knowledge's wallet once more.
The big subscription is running out; the renewal offers are fewer and far between.
O, *Elle*, let me leaf through your semi-autonomous anaesthesia,
so vigorous on the eye, sing *cuccu*!
Look up, around, back, forward if you can take the time, as the seasonal
    smooches turn to pecks.
Winter, I love you still, trying as you can sometimes be with your defensive weather,
but vows are vows.
Here's what the justice of the peace said at my leisurely wedding:
"Repeat after me, though if you are uncomfortable repeating after me, you can pass."
That wasn't my real wedding, rather just a performance work.
Like time itself, which someone said was a river, but it's really merely time, which is
just an idea,
but a heavy one, no f-ing shit.
The months stream on, and I think I'm going to faint.
On the drive to work the other day, I noticed someone had changed the sign
"Skunk River" to "River Acheron".
I would like to think that was a high school prank executed
by some AP English kids.
Anyway, all my bats are in a row, hanging like teardrops in need of a shave,
dreaming of the stars firing down on menacing ducks spitting interest-charge
    fine print
over the phone, and while I wait to have my real concerns addressed, I think
when I grow up I want to be a lay sage, hedging my remarks
in torn relief at the foot of obscure monuments peopled by chafed heroes,
wondering about the stone underwear under all the pomp.

5.

Existence, you are the champion again this bright morning.
Night was another long chance operation, another dream scuffle
between fire and hail, obscurity, desire and denial
(I'd toss in some more specific dream imagery here but none remains, just the
    after-loathing

infectious as eternity sucking the life out of my happy soul's trite lies,
its gentleness falsely recalled and conjured back once more).
It must have rained; the mud below my window is gleaming truth.
I'm as sorry as the sesame seed is oblivious
to the unattainably supreme, to the Absolute
turning on me like the tired gimmickry
of enjambment.
Morning means a fresh start,
so I'll not mess with the décor of your expectations,
with the proper unfolding of the poem as we have come to appreciate it
in all its diversity,
nor will I toy with the brakes and accelerator in the heavy traffic of meaning.
I'll refrain today from acting like a poet savouring the slippage of sense
and the proper phrasing of alienation felt, say, shopping
while grief-stricken for shoes that roar at robins and grackles
like the echo of dead steel plants.
These are the years of rough drainage, similes clogging the pipes of the mind's condo
like teaspoons deliberately shoved by the priesthood down the garbage disposal
   of doubt.
Even weak art has its moments, most of the time.
If it pleases you I'll hop the next train.
I like trains.
I'm open to removal, but only to a place even more openhearted.
Of course I love you, you need love!
Here we all are, in the middle of things once more.
The half-moon slides forth on its less than persuasive course,
and I long for summers past full of love and irresponsible shenanigans, don't you?
Knowledge hisses at me every summer,
tells me to be like a wolf drinking from unrhyming streams spraying past
   scented clover.
Speaking of texts, soon the next invoice will arrive in the mail,
with the rugged and wide Sublime singing its trademark subsonic song
as I open the envelope and examine the charges.
But that's fine.
At least I'll still be here, able to flee or stay,

listening for the next call of the katydid,
revisiting notions of form and anti-form that feed our understanding
of fishy ideals lost on the elk beneath the aspen trees,
not to mention the brains of the great dead philosophers,
their incantations, preambles and bootless packages long-shredded
in the magic boneyard we call existence.

6.

Mum's the word
for the flower known as the chrysanthemum,
the shortened form,
the word not the flower.
And mum's the word for my British mother
in my former life as royal subject,
and mum's the word for the strong beer she liked to swill
in her days as a mummer, but I'll say no more on this.
I thrive amid dozing, so sweet dreams.
You might be interested in this.
I've been to Dylan Thomas's writing shack,
overlooking, as it happens, a green bay that particular day.
In my journal I wrote:
"My shutter-hinge harmonies fail to live long in the gull's whispered reassurances."
I found his grave then retired to the pub for a whisky or two.
It was a Sunday morning and they were not supposed to be open at that hour.
I was young but felt otherwise.
Life is an old rug.
I'll go on my way once this poem is through and so will you,
tapping into your own ingrained melodies and flow or jolt or drag of ideas, emotions.
It's been a long time since I cried, I mean really wept, but it'll happen again
most likely, like sleep falling into the arms of tonight,
which reminds me.
I am as puzzled as the familiar is rampant.
But when you ask me what I'm thinking,
I'd say, "Basilica."

"Tell me more," said my shrink.

"OK. You remind me of a toaster and your dismissal of my own take

is no match for that grizzly bear coming out of my backcountry dreams

with that sepia look of empire in its eyes."

So much for those days, those sessions lost in the flood.

I'm off to chase snails in the dog-eared dew, my fear shifting like sand

whispering, "Shh, shh, you don't love me, I know, but who the hell does?"

I bear no vengeance.

No more than the next mason,

for whom enclosure is a tired place like America

in its red, white, and blue plaid winter cap with earflaps

next to worthless in the vast cold of the vapidly diverted world

inside and external to Connecticut and Saturn.

These formulations can weary one.

Whoosh. Zip it. I've given up on poise,

having wasted too much time envisioning an end to clichés

like reading to be better read.

Tonight, Greenwich remains Greenwich, and Kansas is still Kansas.

Though change unfolds before us (and after).

I hear my grandfathers were quite the critics, no fun,

which leaves me marvelling at the miracle of segue deep in the snowdrifts of
    science

sent dissolving into the dusk.

7.

A few more things you need not know about me.

February is my least favourite month.

I grew up in Iowa and that may be why

with winter's dull throb just about to do us all in in the dirty snow that is love

in the end.

I grew my first beard at the request of an early beloved.

She was fond of quoting Chinese philosophers.

The day I told her I loved her, she replied, "As Lao Tzu says,

'Silence is a source of great strength.'"

It was a lazy summer afternoon and we were drinking wine under our favourite tree
down by the Raccoon River.
Near that spot is a glade.
I still go there one day every autumn and read some of my favourite poems
from the T'ang Dynasty,
shaking off my foolishness of the past year,
feeling somewhat responsible for the suffering I may have caused others.
Memory is pernicious sometimes.
A hickory nut, in and of itself (whatever that means) is not.
I'm not a sellout because I have nothing to sell.
The vast majority of peas I have eaten in my life were frozen.
I miss all my departed cats.
I still like the world enough to stay in it.
It's one hell of an object.
It is disturbing how much dosh is required to reside here.
A yellowed copy of tonight will be slipped under your door later.
It will look like a song written by scary monsters who have no regard
for rights and permissions.
The branches, heavily salted with moonlight, will sway like youth itself,
the point of which is continually difficult to unpack,
given all the slight premises wound tightly as all the ambitious incidentals.
Meanwhile, greed, however fired in the kiln of representation and rhetorical
   assumption,
writes itself its own ticket, as we used to say.
I come before you, shut down like summer's recognizable end,
walled off from the echo of the erased word, yet continuous
as the peaks poking into a new day of history's indulgences
and the next poem on the move in the immediate depths of bygone years
green as the vast sleeve of the trees unable to scratch the stars
unlike the imagination.
Phone it in, that's fine.
Who's telling you otherwise?
The collective voice of the pumpkins of Michigan?
Obscurity is actually sweeter than all the pathetic splash filling the house organs
pumped out by the organizations we work for,

as true mystery swirls in the flat-panel glow
captive as the dust on a thousand aging bottles
promising downed wisdom.
This is the content and this is the package.
I guess hope lives, hopes live as the meaning of the world undoes itself,
no matter its intentions,
according to some thinkers,
their names less important than the idea cooking off
like the sherry in the overwrought sauce of language.

8.

"I've got your brilliant new novel right here," I typed, then paused
to look out at the cracked parking lot in the early dawn.
Christie upstairs is having work done on her kitchen,
and I know the noise will begin in three hours and I will
not have slept enough.
I can't fathom
the horror that is likely my mother's inner life
as she sits through her wait for death, resenting me as always,
that resentment her glimmer of meaning in the darkening clamour
of her cave of dementia and general bodily demise.
Tomorrow, or really, later today, we move her to the next level of "care" at the
    retirement "village."
Laugh if you want to, but the immutable pose of all the vanished drama in the
    known universe
dawdles like you and your conscience, like the dribble of citric acid gleaming
kitty-corner to the lack of distance between you and your mores.
Read 'em and bleep.
I'm better off just remembering
to pretend I didn't get the memo
on how to operate the new entryway keypad intercom system at my condo, since…
Long (or semi-long) story.
I don't expect you to follow much of what I say without further explanation.
Yes, you in the shadow of the descending blimp.

What are my views on artistic originality?
Well, I find the discussion tired and old, I mean
it's, like, choose your thing and just do it,
just do it well, I say, it's pretty much all been done before, or something close
    enough to it,
someone will appreciate it if you're lucky and if not, screw it.
True, I tend to begin conversations with people as if we've been talking for
    some time.

Fourmi

I'm getting older,
far from nothing and
that's cool, a bit cool,
as I turn up my collar
amid some momentary
abstruseness too early,
just ask wisdom
trailing out front
of the shadow of the act,
treading river's song
in ignorance,
in all known darkness,
dismiss me.
Fine. I'll try
to wake gladly
to the world's reduction,
face the speakers
pushing on this heart's
fading work,
as the listing pines
promise no lies,
no song,
gentle as the year
coming ten thousand years on.
Love, ticking,
no moaning,
to be read
beneath these words
tuning up another
town full of shrapnel,
yeah, right, scented, stop.

Yes, what's
the other tune?
Unknowing as
the ale of the dead,
the well-read
open to rising
out of the brown earth
that entails
the expansive collage
of fear,
creatures suffering glazed
in the old pan,
soul's kiss of grist,
of kindly given mysteries
reflecting on the finish
of spring's familiar
and tasty acts of light.
Lead me
out of the noise
and back into the noise,
but first let's review
what sides doubt refuses
to take,
the market's
oracular crawl,
mocking the ancients
striding about
in the latest robes,
back-slapping each other's
paradoxes.
It is apparent.
I'll continue
to piece together
something sure,
some narrow

specialization bequeathed
by a million dreaming experts
raining down
like lilac tumbleweeds,
sages of the lonely earth,
what more can I add?
A dying bouquet
of selfhood?
I'll keep seeking the central
motif of the innumerable,
forget it.
Mother of my feelings,
relieve me
of my dusty symptoms,
hawk me a fresh start.

*

Some late summer rain
showering city-haze dust
from yellowing leaves,
I suppose—
suchness needs a nap.
Humid afternoon—
lone monarch,
fluttering low
in long pine-shadow.
Seconds tick away,
a tick comes back
for seconds and
this time:
bye for good.
September unfurling—
sunflowers flashing
in the afternoon wind,
apples and honey;

look out for more firepower.
Shredded spiderweb.
Rush hour traffic jam—
drifting across my windshield:
downtown thistledown.
Nothing new there,
here, just a reminder
to keep the old mind
open.
OK, OK, OK,
OK, OK, OK, OK,
OK. O!
Chipmunk sniffing
a fallen walnut,
darting off—
too big a nut to crack.
Archipelago of geese
flying south, semi-forming
the V-sign we seek.
Coming soon enough
the first hard frost—
please, a light one first,
just asking.
A thought came to me.
It was not an autumn thought.
Though it was autumn,
thought rotting through
me, not autumn-wrought
sodden thought—
hardy autumn rot,
though hardly, really,
who are we kidding,
mind thought.
Love, myth,
brain-flare, bog.

"Moon, setting in the west,
thanks for last night's eclipse."
"It was nothing."
Wild turkey
on the river sandbar—
the bird
not the booze;
high school's done.
Dear ill lumberjack,
Hope you are felling better.
Take care,
Not a Tree.
Codeine suppression—
sleep so I can
go to work tomorrow,
coughing.
Lost my credit card then found
my lost credit card. Missing, then,
not lost. You
destabilize then ask
why it's all so, so
unstable? Good one.
My nails need clipping.
How about some paper,
a pencil, natural light,
write a short poem?
Layoffs first,
then surprise!
Surpluses pop up,
wow!
Welcome to the club.
A chill
once more:
in the diminishing light,
fleeting wisdom reigns.

Popcorn radical
dapper equestrian
husk.
Sharply cold
morning, cold as
this aster petal.
Burn ban in effect statewide—
the oak tree flames
in place.
Schlocky bright leaf,
there's no such thing as you, kid,
keep doing your thing.
Still life:
my neighbour's porch—
scarecrow, pumpkin, sleeping cat.
The cat's name is Alfred.
No. I don't think so.
I could be wrong, yes,
but still.
Traffic jam on the bridge.
Look up river:
blue heron wisp wading.
Lien's daybed,
nasal, spent effigy
of magic,
pre-mixed gadabout.
Pumpkin's carved
and lit on the eve
of All Saints' Day—
"Some kugel?"
"Sure."
What time is the thing?
You know,
the thing that's tonight.
The thing! Remember?

Singularity? Individuality?
Fictionality? The sun's gone away,
not yet.
Some branches bare now,
some full red,
orange, yellow,
some still
leafy green.
Avoiding cliché—
light cascading
through my sneeze,
tears falling
like elves.
Stood in the aviary,
reading my tweets aloud—
some racket!
My Swiss Army Knife
is folded up
and ready
for neutral action.
Write something
each day?
No, it doesn't work
that way.
Life says "hush"
at times.
Leaf blower, shut up,
fuming brute,
overkiller
of this still morning.
The neighbour's car alarm
woke me
ahead of my clock,
out of dreamed star-snow.
Which means, which means, which

means I can't say,
don't know,
no, whatever,
silence
flowing, flowing—
humankind's flaming stream—
from bloodshed to
bloodshed to...
the days carry on,
carry us on,
routines, smiles,
nagging, nagging hope.
This winter had to come,
this snow, wet, thick,
drenched white "blanket",
a sopping blanket,
great memories.
Down in the valley—
the train whistle blows
a nameless mood
up my way.
I've been asked
to share
my thanks publicly,
profoundly, or else.
Low clouds wrangle,
my out-of-office reply
awaits its mission.
Need to bookmark
the book
I'm currently reading—
cold, grey, bells chiming,
bright future approaching,
land of
opportunity.

Bullets abound.
Trimmed the old
Christmas tree—
three years old—
old under capitalism.
Nightfall sang to me:
"Sang"?
More of a croak.
Meeting's coming up—
no docket full of posies—
drone on, thorn weeds, skulls.
"Another cookie?"
"No, I'm good,
one is enough."
Truth for the belly,
lie of the tongue.
Headed to the pub
for dinner, ale, ye olde
replications.
Years ago,
in the Scottish wind—
my mother
at St. Andrews
barred from the clubhouse.
The server brought our stout,
too warm.
T-shirt said:
"Try one now, ice cold."
Memories present...
memories, present
presence, open mind's presents?
When I was young
I dreamed of presents.
The dream of presence
floated later.

Presenting the next poem
about absence...
wait for it,
wait for it, wait...
settling nothing.
Vaporous torpor—
vacuous stupor, jingling
all the way.
Christmas lights
shimmering through
my rain-streaked windows.
"What detergent did you use?"
my wife asks,
dreaming.
Your gleanings
slip free,
briny peelings, anyway
forget it all, expanse.
Constructions shimmy,
funny, no?
Say more,
keep humming,
bright morn, bright quiet,
caress of noon's
low-seared silence.
Light snow
blowing through—
a few flakes
on my shoe, gone.
Your hurry, flurries?

*

The flowers found it hard
to love the buildings.
The concrete shadows,

while predictable,
could not be trusted.
Still, talent jumped forth
in living colour:
purples, yellows,
violet of course.
It is difficult to
cuddle up with all
your thoughts
until the hour
of mercy or no mercy
scrapes the walls
of the heart
like a bag of
avocado oil potato chips
munched on
by the mouth beside you
in the minutes before
your lunch order arrives.
Would you
rather be doing
something else
just now?
That's OK.
I mean, who doesn't
want the troops
to come home?
They should come home
and the powerful
should just go out
and whack some mushrooms
with their walking sticks
in the humid dawn
like our
dragon-fearing

ancestors of old.
The hard and soft piano
of poetry
will not make
anything come true
except the hardness
and softness
of the piano's poetry.
Even then, nothing
is certain.
The space you're in
is like a hotel:
temporary home to joy,
heartbreak, jealousy,
dead fashion.
The truth is the wealth
I've had to tolerate
can't cherish
the sweet grace
of light in the grass.
If you put
the right knives on
the table
for the meat you plan
to serve, the entire economy
of phantom production
will respond
with record growth
and reduced inspiration.
Don't you just love the music
you can't hear right now?
Be a cactus.
You look like a cactus
so it's not a stretch.
I mean that as a compliment

because I love most cactuses.
I am plural.
Just look at the night.
You are plural too.
Silence asks
for a moment of calm
unlike science.
And that's
probably good for us all.
The clouds
keep coming and going,
like the light,
even when your
shirt collar is lit,
with formality.
The funny thing is,
so much is funny,
except if you're a snail,
for we can only assume
that a vast majority
of creatures
miss out on humour.
Isn't that sad?
At least they don't
have to worry
about ad copy and
opera profits.
Studies show
that red swimsuits
exude wealth,
caution,
a recent history of ambition,
and dampness
when wet.
I don't know

any other way to put this.
It's like trying to
wade across the lagoon
without looking clumsy.
Talk about a rat race.
To think that I
jumped right in
when I was young
and seeking what was steady,
exciting, bouncy,
and fun.
My favourite mountain
remains a craggy touchstone
in my imagination.
Who are we?
Nothingness darkens
like the trees
still hanging out
in my childhood neighbourhood
long before and after me.
Circus. Laughter. Wine. Tomorrow.
I am waiting for
the sea to rush in.
It will sound like applause
because
tonight it's
slaphappy and marvellous
like love's joy
coming to rest
with a promise to rally.

Vates

I

Beauty! Crickets!
      Look at you, out attending to your next abstract state—*Oui!*
I'm new to the professionalism.
              What's missing in the afternoon sun? Insignificance?
Gather and advise. Develop your insouciant
              theories.
Spicy as the past some nights after ten.

Later follows remarkably in the not-so-tonely spray of early patience.
We're on it, and through, perhaps stark in our borrowing of blighted memories.
What a day.
Has the next saint pondered a robin, authorless text, fresh faces in the oak bark,
maybe ghost-prairies?
I am coming apart in the wider sense, in my usual cockamamie way, though this time a bit
   time a bit
horizontally like a scar forming the shiny shadow of a feather on my forehead.

II

Spell of the slightly to dare.
Father about in the almonds again.
All hands in town playing
shake those poems.
That's Wales washing
up the windows.
Shattering of the A-world.
Burn breeze measure.
I lead along fear,
you autumnally remember
the mercury vapour.
All whole, known drainage, golly,
perhaps, college once a holiday of casual doubt.
Here in mind's nothing new here...

III

Sedated by
the world's coarse melody
once more, I'm
dimly lit in mystery, shiftless
amid the grey apologies,
the apples shredded
like the hopes of sages.
An intermittent hiss
gloms summer's chipped ex-profile.
Hey, get used to it, my friend. How 'bout a lightning round of "Captain, May I?"
Copernicus aches no more
for scrimpy pay.
Couplets are fun for some, for others not.
Too rough to hear vague time come
slantly wrought,
come landing here and there and
to the right?
The value of a varied oomph is felt as necessary, as a happy diversion. Just
   saying. Sighing. Yes,
have another difference.

IV

Before I was leaf dust, I was a leafy haven dubbed America.
The wolf reads refusal, efficiency, principles in the glorious parkway skirting true
    connection.
Don't speed. The spaces don't lie. Lapses sometimes do. Help.

At last you are washing out your preferences, I repeat, go ahead and relish
your own tabloid fantasies, it's a free country, to hell with you, heck, with us all.
This page lacks herd mentality unlike the sceptics roaming the avenues for waxy
    produce.

I'll remain here, despising the elephant in the lounge.
That would be living in the real world of sirens, researchers, homey thinking and
    volunteers
handing out bookmarks to backpackers and starving farmers who have no
    associations with Westport.

Note to file: I'm not back on top because I was never on top.
Doctoring my view by shutting the window as dawn seeps through, blue as it
    comes.
Devotion playing its hand.

The gardener in me sleeps. Let me explain. Form is a thought-bug.
Summer offers up another trifle of a radio hit, our latest yellowing escape late-sprung
from the pageless book of whatever.

V

What stalls in thought's long-narrowed, streamless eaves is transient as the bother coursing now through truth and heart held fast to mind's blunt prow. Just go on home to rain and sodden leaves; exchange the open days left to perceive what passing cares impassively allow... perhaps I'm merely fogging up the slough. False measures cloud the songless core in droves. I scratch and wonder how to keep all ripe. Perhaps a walk around the block will clear the head, undo the madcap jam that comes and goes like shredded meaning in our sleep. Remember those ideas you dreamed so dear? It's been some time since I enjoyed a plum.

VI

praise euphony—
what I heard

or was it

fired up (at any rate), solid as any bard gone
prismatic in the flow of absence, in the shadows of the cold-coded city of
   shredded has-been
   selves, trashed cartons flapping in the wind, shouldering a lack of correspondences.
      Something's changed along the long line of thinking to feeling to remembrance,
         long, that is, as one particular stretch of the ceaseless.
               blow of applied
         rustlings outside my hut of... knowledge:
      store is to pineapple as intuitional world is to passive kicks baked at close range
   Out with it and in through the gate of wanting, of textual glaze.
   More famous doings? Big spills?
... proximate as youth's sunny comments, moist faces maintaining mock floral
      candelabras... drained minds, limber as the Lord skipping up and down
   steps unswept by
   summer's after-school pleas

Hello,
reflected in the shop windows, layered into me like need
chattering down the alleys, stylishly crammed, wall-to-wall.
quarrelling as usual about security with the smart-asses,
enduring billboard prayers, living
imprecisely, hearing, as one does,
another aura calling among the leaves in the ditches of wisdom...

the short of it:
      one aluminium broke new strokes

latest of merely on or say and off to
      shattering wit, solitude, jewellery, a rush heard coursing through
     my cornucopian whys
    three utterances thousands and one organism's latest kiss, on with the
blessings and
   that's all
      get out

The hair dryer in my hotel room came with an advisory tag:
"Do not remove: warn children of the risks of death by electric shock"
... and of course death by firearms here in God's peaceable kingdom of liberty
  and justice
   for...
Don't start, I said to myself. Write a haiku. Go metaphorical. Do both:

plump up the pillows,
go for the biggest cushion,
watch the leaves falling

(so I plumped up the pillows/went for the biggest cushion/and vowed to watch
     the next red leaf fall)

VII

It's loving glade formulation, lot making
was as destiny in abstract
pose up and eat like you mean to treat
the lawn as the great thesis it isn't.

Write, lush thought and sing the songs
of bone and maybe hair, pretty as the east testing desire
in the winds of fun spidering to kill,
shuffling the sets, sound amid
the moths bristling and bracing for help.

You're the you in application notice
some dream:
to each the "little" abuses pass for air—tiny blah...
and with sat as fields shaved in mourning
partnering collectively prior to the fall.

Once into earnestness, feeling loads, hit internally by sleep.

In place: a stadium full of readers, stationary as their books kept elsewhere for
   another day.

Say yes to lightning lighting up the page as you left it last:

... of the first in say shape steams the first point of the drink, remembrance...
These are words written deep in the machinery of the moon.
      but by   like the vital upon
         your which off faces that's like of once do harmless
      take my lapses out like
please we can written milk-cracked weights,
            summer's too understanding believed the if if the and was
         for believing some offer.

VIII

You work and you whisper, "How is it going?"
But the mortgaged beads of conflict
direct the next kiss to shut one song down,

one turn from the rotation coming through the walls
in tiny gusts, fodder along the way for the writer,
whose shadowed glare weaves a truth only the cheapest guitar could fret.

in tight is the "it" thought, the face of Frisco's *moi* down oven
could you know
the half of it eternally lost like
another page of substantial

lift loss and build yourself a towering
is but always a cream its holiday of life the like further morning about the again
eyes from comparatively
poem strung out on universals
ruined force, accruals, asks autumn away beyond dream gritty say centre of
   the days with that
   enduring forms worn up
no material match
collection to
all the looking as
itself.
the look watch that for felt frame feel to book summer
on of fileted, in translation: stars flick atheist raised melody and aside identity

                    those thinking worked
you desk
idling drop—
what so dank the up
in want is they

I super arms the over anvilized,
the full big my and of lawn
the shore
pinching Camus
And?
It freezes somewhere, much like my low-blowing memory clouds of Madrid
next to thought's remaining jay hiding in the bush quivering in the rush
of nearby locomotion.

Speed is mythological,
certain as my years in New Amsterdam,
where need was its own borderless capital
and happiness brought me down
many evenings to the foyer of dispersed roaming,
remaining amiss, free as a poem out to lunch
on its internship at the firm of Attention, Pine, Country, and Waste.

IX

what can I add to what's been said so far?
the glow the stain the splintering all   you feel
when young your friends outshone the brightest star
the icy lane at night shines like an eel
the gleanings multiply slip uncontained
constrictions laughing loud between your ears
you've little new to sing in sun and rain
"this too shall pass" so dry those lug-nut tears!
in dreams tight forms give way to looser joy
and don't you know it   don't you shake your head
order   OK   but whose do we deploy?
the shadowed grooves of sacred scribes long dead?
such stress I guess assess obsess god bless?
hold fine in light's unfailing ceaseless mess

X

Much to plug, much to unplug.
The feel of the light is open and about.
Another?
Late-summer lit, I comb my hair and write up the reverberating formulas.

You take the years' words as improbable as the town's slobbering alignments.

Famous only slightly in the mind.
Twist, pull out a few tyrants from the heap of their own making?
Raw and on the mend?
Caravaggio's out-of-tune song dialogues with the ideal and death.

The way to do more of this is don't.
The dismissive sheen of the frost arises like serviceable questions of ancient
    thought.
The stench of all this contemporary creativity... whence my old Underwood?
Of the other, of the then, where in the distance turns aswirl the notion?
Peacocks. Just peacocks. I mean peaches I mean peppers.
We're all just trying out the latest week in the wind, despairing that we can't say
much more about the usual.

Mention decline and watch me accept a chance to see the island departing.
Send a nice beautiful wave my way, you bloodless rabbit.
Sorry to be so demanding.
You pick the tile, the backsplash.
Thought I held the best cards and then I was delivered the news
of the unexpected layover.

Spotty love? No, this is all about the self.

America 24/7 sell-calmed in anyway one broken E. T. fox across ending
    hammer survival.

Professors, speed your denial of transcendence from the aisles to the graveyard.
I don't know, what, nickels?

Could blow psychedelic, cliché as a whale of a plunge.

O.

XI

That noise was the wind (not the noise in the wind).
Grandma, who can blame you for your...
       who at carts hot on read
For your disdain of my experimentation.
Which grandma?
Money flows in as I write this but not much.
Nothing, something, lonely, I peel.
Oxford is reliable.
Lorry beauty.
Square and old as Virginia amid the canned lands of shadows sliding
slow as a song symbolizing something contained
in your human step, right?
Vanishing remarkably in response to the pace.
Anyway, the dead of night would like some tea.
Weak form, weak formlessness, really, poetry?
Really, everything, for that matter.
Cosmos as yawning maw.
Your professional achievements, your contributions to the splinter of nothingness
that is your sniping profession sniping, well, I'm sorry for your gain.

XII

How about it, more of a grin, eh?
You are no mayfly and you know how it feels to love.
Why the return, a mere seconds past closing the books on September?

Dead free not tired or high as the Pyrenees spirited
semi to France sometime back.
Three days at sea, sudden as an envelope.
The takeaway: the takeout could have been better.

Writing is a fine way to repeat yourself.
Talking, not so much.
Poems? Only if feathered-up and fewer than never advised.

Regard being.
Stuck to the train.
Time to regret?

On the great ladder of beloveds past, where doth your favourite bird perch
to view the lake, to not know the kitchen and all its recipes of argument
echoing, the parchment-wrapped faces of history muffled, steaming?

How strong is the future, how much further to carry the load,
to tarry like a toad?
Stop 'em. Ponder like _____ would in the doped-up glare of his
second coming.
Composure is nothing to laugh off, hah!

You are you and your psychological certainty ripples wildly
like a bag full of literary allusions spilled on the brûléed sidewalk
offering nothing
to the haiku masters colliding on the avenue, big deal, leave off now,
spitting shale stars into your phone.

XIII

Footprints in the snow—
Old image, fresh morning snow.
You get the picture.
Memory, how have you been?
Cooler than hell!

Last and yes, to evening hiker uncurled,
    like but just with about balanced to after we are yet from October.
Baked mow parabola.

I took the fall and
bookmarked rigor's punch as
you chewed the fat and rued the
baseless hunch.

Discernment's carnival made promise not to end; this strange and passing
  timelessness
undoes the rhyming pen.

XIV

Yeah? Grow up, and spare me your cartoonish quarrels.
The people are following through on their threat of extinction.
Show yourself. I see you hiding above the hovering peaks.
Callow. Naïve. Inexpert.
As was our little Attila in his youth, abiding till inspired.
I have half a notion to cross the river and share my passé
self-assessments with a buffalo or two.

XV

The rocks slid in bunches, crumbling like the years of half-arsed work
comprising my dosh-mongering portfolio.
What will be light's last meaning?
This is what the end of knowledge looks like, ideally,
to mannered farmers
short on nursery skills, long on messaging fantasies.
Which is why I fled the green hills of thought, the morning's good eye
literate with rain.
My shirts are in a good place, buttoned down, lightly starched, which is
how my friends describe me.
Clearly a case of projection.
And what of my shoes, feeling the way through the haze that's no match
for the gathering *tramontane* battering my roof.
Hanging eschews ignorance.
Not me grunting in my new tie.
Disarmed waves glimmer-dimple the Rio Foscari.
How's that?

A demand for book-length sense barges in.
Excuse me.

XVI

I replaced the lock so we should be good to go.
The family is a mother to all dreams. Of all dreams?

I am like the rain, undone, rough with the tactics, bat-weary as the ducklings
swimming the flooded streets of Geneva, Nebraska.

Let's embrace.
Let's not overreact to the sultan's wintry baby thing.

Molly. There, I said it, interpret it as you wish.
Perhaps by some miracle just as the founders did.

I was told to remain an enigma—
advice from the hero in the next cubicle.

The front seat had claw marks, so I passed on the purchase.
Fine, be a primordial operative, good grief, but shit-can the

aphorisms, the stupidity, yeah, the hoarfrost, too,
even if only slightly, for money's not the issue,

no, it's a lack of gusto, resistance paid, cool-quilled,
difficulty iced up to subdue the taste of cornmeal

pulled straight from the trash
in the blustery severance blowing me down the road of elders.

XVII

The beauteous library
The studiously lying berry
once
a world to
put one to bed
fast

Let's begin with what came first. Cute *and/but* waylaid, the language of Jesus
though in anger, a touchstone to skirt death, just there, at rest in the yard
behind the garage, remember? My soul is failing, whirring, a flush-red nothing
   to autumn's
increasing wish to not trigger suffering.
Volunteer.
Chime, fixture, blame.
Pastel
    three dignity destiny
  shall, may, down-wear   here's the
                        knew

      it

XVIII

Party like a magazine full of real people.

   Looks the thing.

   I'll treat you to my pulse?

         The Alps have it over noisy warehouses.

        deer easing in the know not struck saved by dispositionals, hah!
  how to fund,
too, an open rebel oozing down meaning's windy back to God here get the
  want free of the forte

  leaf, oh, not so

what remains

Connecticut, talk about your swizzle mouth!   I'm happening, used to jog,
  look at the
       clods of life's earthen mask merely managing,

              perception...

The stars above keep submitting the same manuscript (sort of),
night after night: Excellent!

The work's been previously published, though, and we love it,
      and true, we have the space, OK, you're in again.

Phone, be quiet, be a bone, be bone-quiet...

     here of likely will out Bag as not trail thousand into Letter to for I so the
  principle a few
        porous leeks told to see through clearing—
   summer mustard
on desk valley, sing, provide, I

For the sake of your waste? Repress?

Probably, moist as the stars,
jumping out of the backseat
of the compact
 universe

go in human nowhere for America's jog through the swarm of chirping horseflies

XIX

bedrooms hanging quiet flower angel consciousness takes a nice pinot noir assumes a voice wearing rain I guess time is still heavy pocked the pig has been where bishopric with collapsed chairs a poem's dead scraps coffee per section this exists as night exists leave, gushing for some mothers she need not try reveals the measure's gem notes using certain doings to work out the new the open book once creamed a grudge in the grass O graves thanks existence cheaper I'm there a no-show the days do count dinner keeps a bit well... I could hear the church's roar which one and from where air sand words we've been on the move looking through the linen sheen sans thinking out in the sticks run down truth be told sleeping unlike new babies dreaming of domestic steel feathered counterarguing guesswork egging on the seers I'll find the surly beauty to rid me of wisdom's loop

XX

Fibre-optic nostalgia.
Maybe I can chart a course toward celebration,
in the shadow of the mast of poison time abuzz and leaning slightly.

I'm with the company, not with company.

And I'm dreaming like an auditorium, spewing security like rivers of ponies
   skipping down
the driveway that leads to the equator.

What kind of mind is this?

Parse summer, birds, morning, nothing to buy.

Misfire in the tropics.

Let the town bear its heart on its stratospheric neck,
propped up like a can, cups, a tour, trees
listening to the horoscope of life.

Said head in need of a wrench to the suspect page and what do you hear,
   greenish matter,
a branch extended, a pillow for Beauty's weary and timeless tug-of-war. Easy.

More

Of essays, of the moon, say,
    hotbed form,
shuffler waves
scrambled as the better nails of my nurture...

rain frizz teetering
and a worm slipping down the easement,

    mind full of nothing's prowess
  marvelling at the wild bay long-pooling back of the forehead—

    forgiving crawler of a brain,
  full of leisure, accruals... sweet cageling

Wingless as the graves, leaves on the quay...
    curriculum holes.
  The affray of time shreds dove after dove.

Loitering: written refuge of these gone years swishing free of assists.

    universe deepening
    in-shoes look meaning in
    the smiles fatherless visitation
    ridiculous aswirl
    whispered again
    and a hurried thought yawns
    engaging dreams of eaten chains
    differentiating stylistically

true with exactly
sudden weeks staying the matter

on me within a you that itself
flings the building's ego swoon-side
so predictable, so
complex, the then, the now, the feature,
(the "hmm"—)

     one intersection finds time barging through
     the locks of loving increase,
     light leading us to look up
     to see passing geese
     could say as a friend it all depends
     on meeting our masks head-on,
     on digging the first and last ideas of the day
     adrift, like meaningless certificates after the trend,

lopped marquees
once perched along the avenues
proclivities carried bookishly, funds slipped under the door,
turns the spirit has taken
as more than mere distraction, foci?
 all the swill I have left waxes to song,
     to regather the forgotten,
   as wishes granted dissipate
      under the fetchless stars
       frame another "no" kept by the latest
    way to see—
   apparent crowing all around my house
you say you paid your social dues then danced poorly at the gala?
streets smooching soles, equitable montage
       body-wound, oozing ABCs—
         a mesh of gods it was said they had,
      they held,
         working from sunup to... bullets?
immaculate revealment lining envy's row of scars too frank to aspire to
  shadow memory

rotate, rotate nosing through
words to obscure
the feel of compote—
day sauced with kissed relief
loopy rose, falling now,
jammed with sophomoric psychohistories of form,
prehistoric, buried, hovering above lost trails
I am, as some may have warned you,
small-time, vigorous as a victory lap around the furnace,
dressed in autumn's factoid screen.
countered, ordained privately
with tears adrip in the thicket, anything else?
Solitude, contrarian apse, doors open to a cardinal's summer gravity—
the polarities are missing from the postcards from Bordeaux.
spirited-in exchanges, spatial, bleary as the young miller...
the adventurer Eternity smiles, bellies up to the puritanical
with longing for clarity... closure
Contentment can wait, like a grungy fill line.
It seemed a severed and fadeless theory after all,
blotch-pronc, juicier one moment
then greying with palmy bits of sky's erasure.
I called to a hum
in the wind.
The wind blew, the dam harmonized,
and flurries skirted the day.
mix of wishes,
real, simple, spare...
positively to see amid another
great budding expiration of mind's
singing pestilence
lost just this side
of anyway, translations
from the noble to the executive
reaching wryly for wilier vistas
Knowing had its moments, imagining its freedom from yuck drooping from

the grate. The cravings did not die.
Mere days to full indulgence;
      yesterday's cares contracted a thesis.
            Kicked in: the watchful yaw of hope despising heads.
Project transcendence? I guess this is
the road past the bluing ache, negligible, all aglow.
Quiet? Power?
Shine up the take before it drags like the sons of floating babble.
                  Oh, in just the
      produce shouldn't cracks
        souvenir night and a tougher new insisted
                  we of in sneeze for
                  at save your nowhere unseen.
        you were off, to be feted in the lunar highlands,
         and persistence may freak hourly beneath mobile asks... I am?
   taught wilfully deep with predictions,
        no, I wasn't, unlike _____.
   I'm not a job, not a bawlin' bawdy left, real, co(u)ld...
      poured into moth-eaten cups
   playing a chalky way-dead
river's silt trilling
the frost squeaks: being checks itself at some level,
      mid-afternoon, once and evermore or still
revelatory, born extinctualzing melody...
            around a where sweeping new makes more bubbles
astonishing, his spumy peals,
      hiked down saviour-mode
        on paper or streaming
steady hues
   of awesome, woesome
            I needed a ripple, received silence...

Yarner

I

Yardage forgotten, solstitial fade, as I reimagine that old severing song leading me to polka right out of ballroom dance class. Ginsberg offered a spontaneous revision to one of my haiku. Sure.

Got a postcard from the Sandhills. Turned it into a found poem: "Everything's fine and dandy. / Bought myself a mobile home. / Two bedrooms, living room, the works. /All worn out from digging a ditch / 5 feet by 25. / Fell into it last night in the dark. / Shit. / Write soon. / B." To be clear, America is not my favourite summer movie (things passing in and out of the mind, mind passing in and out of things). Unfair work—that is, the empire—stretched right on through evensong.

With my in-laws, looking for their ancestors in an English graveyard, watching a young family load into their car, I thought of an idea for a short story. The title: "Writing is a Form of Discovery". A man discovers he is not the moon, possessing, as he always has, a bad sense of chronology, a scratchy faith in kismet, an indifference to Keats's "Bright Star", and, like most, a pedestrian sense of oneness.

Again a general cry: the past eight hours! Thanksgivings (oh please!)! And lately? Just hanging at Cap d'Ail. Year's end, more Googlism, mileage, meaning, lonely, lonely. Hey! The sublime's fogging to blue, a distillation of roses, knowledge in review, grand allusions filling the French triptych smeared with tankas in drippy translation.

To wit, t' tweet, to whom it may concern. Sing it. *Bah oui.* Creative nonfiction followed me from Savannah to Charleston. Welcome (better late than...). On the cab ride to the Camelback Inn Resort and Spa, I spun for the cabbie my now forgotten Killarney Trilogy.

Words listing, I tried to remain upright, riffing another intro, a morning in May exercising fragments, good interpretations, a memoir of one autumn and its remembrance of faux horse sense. Please pass the cookies. Marvellous. And the *vin ordinaire*.

Echovox stew: meaning matters, before and after and back at you doling out Benjamins like comparisons trumping loosey-goosey, still projecting memories of the latest shooting in sonnet form, cutting across the OK panhandle in the paisley seashore rain, proverbs glowing red and gold in spring's promising air. Must be the beans. Or Dad's favourite golf balls bouncing around the interior of the old noodle. Pick up the pen and call it a poem, not an institutional rubric, filler like success, a testamental ambience, a selfie earnest as the treasury of emptiness, variation in the wind yapping. Zurpreeze!

A gathering erasure of firsts strewn along Hackney Pass. How to know precisely how the memo's useless distraction fouls the pin's fall into the bin. Tuppence for your thoughts? Well, just the sorry boom of ye olde avant-garde, a shouldering of pesky trite tropes.

II

# #

Turn out the artefacts of your imagination. Tea? illspreoogud. ; ; ature. Hark!
Back to some steaming order?

Crawling from my solarium to my data turret,
I went in search of the nightmare's measurable outcomes.

train whistle blowing in thick fog, echoing up the river valley a third-tone
higher, muted

I read the critical introduction explaining
what is going on in the work.
I annotated the sunrise slipping across the page.

I may be addressing you soon,
fair thoughts for the fair,
procedural sludge for the decimators.

Feeling mixed, a bit of alachrymosity
as I count the embedded chimes springing through June foliage.

Waiting for that singular narrative to emerge, endlessly revisable,
worthy of memory's revisitation, I
framed the present.

Gathered some lavender and white phlox... and now on my sox
I've got burrs that clingle-tangle-stingle.

Cool it. Going nowhere. Like the apple that rolled a promising distance from
the pear tree. Like the toss that sent it further, into the chaparral.

Why the tyre-swing doubt?

I'll trust the pattern in the rope, the weave,
the braid, the tale.
Nascence tells me something
is still quaking in the lost meadow
on the cutting room floor.
Eternity, I apologize for all the cuckoo figuration.

Hastening to find some peace of mind, I'm up.
Understandably sweaty.
Maybe I'll return to the fading climate of wonder.
I watch the haze hang.
Dry winter endurance, forgotten scratch.
Imitation's theatrics yawn.

tree-trunk shadow—drooling a squirrel

#

At The Lucky Duck gastropub we see no duck on the menu but of course that's
why they call it The Lucky Duck—cheers!

A fly lands on the handwritten page I am typing up,
less obtrusive than my remembered cat.
It will only take a wave of my hand
to send the fly on its way.

The shoe that was on the other foot has now dropped—after some effort.

Brushed a croissant flake from my trouser leg—
before a butter stain could set in.

The sparkling lights of Nice at night across the bay
have given way
to the sparkling morning sea—
as Black Sabbath's "Hole in the Sky" plays in my head.

Idling, we encounter the road ahead:

three signals:
red, yellow, flashing yellow:
two directions down to one lane:
no green.
And from behind, a weedwacker of a motorbike speeding past.

through the canicular haze: snow-streaked Alps

Got a jolly reprimand—got a real cheerful.

Sapped of light and patience for the itch to resolve,
we caught the coast lining through the haze and stupefying heat.
The level sea, pine, palm, tourterelle, gull's bark, diesel, rampart ruin—
the tableau of morning offers a fine napkin to wipe away the dirt of ardour.

"How are you today?"
"Fine, can't complain, no use complaining anyway, I mean, no one's listening."
"Did you say something?"
"I said—."
"Yes, I heard you. Just a little joke."
"Yes, a little one."
"Have a nice day."
"Another joke. 'Nice day.' You're a funny one."

#

Love made me want to cry like a ladle dripping acid fog.

Cold as... mice. Dead, test-rattled mice. Cat-rattled? No. Keep it human.

Though once true at heart,
the youthful enthusiasms felt now like distant fictions,
delusions.
Any gleam off the fossil, artificial.
I begged the lily to shadow me through the highlands.
The narrows of attachment proved easily cast.

75

Harrowed to the last.

I stand supplanted in the clearing, in the heraldry of sun and stone, a shiftless
relic eked from aught.

Guessing as always, I follow the lost eclogue balancing before nebulous ease.
Rail, yaw, as we must.

As the monuments rot in the pale rushes, the drafts of indolence dim the turn to
inward solace. Supple revelry. Supplicatory. Applicable. Billable neglect. Needlework.

The air bluffs composure, fleet as honey.
The jewel found in the knapsack shines its naysayer's music.
Open, peony bud, we cannot help thinking.
Quarried.
Time upstages a whiff of Xanadu.
What a wind. What a zeal-zoned moment.

Late summer afternoon—an owl hooting—
on the lookout for an early bird special?

All leeward these leanings, roughing up
the dimming afterglow, shed, deciduous as sanity.
Levity enrages. Almost dawn.
Time scuffs the overwrought you in youth.
Apropos, out to pasture,
no pie dish in the sky pooling rain either.
Care insinuates an aperture,
a tithing
of effortless chirping.

Comfort, oscillating most frivolously, outraged rhetoric's tambourine. Zoning
optics neutralized effervescence.

What to expect. A dry field,

mole mounds, stone cross stretched in pale grass,
keep your eyes on your path, your way across,
look out for dog shit.
Do a little quickstep,
quirkstep, quiet as the stardust in the blade, as sunlight on skin.

It's not a lack of this but of that that's causing it. A lack of that but this. While this.
You are busier than you think, which is why you forgot to finish reading that
must-read. Must be it, must be the reason, you tell yourself as if you were two.

In the flow of it. Dreams free of recent hauntings. Ghosts in the old family home
just up the hill. Why did you buy a place so close? You weren't thinking? Live for
the swim beneath the cliffs, the trees. Live for many reasons. Now you are thinking.

We still have plenty of cereal for breakfast. No need to thaw the muffins just yet.
If the manual says to hold the button for three seconds, that means three
seconds, not a quick count of three. Evasive answers return in several layers of
erasure.

Unintended meaning of
something you said occurring. Power
just went out. It's back.
What was I saying?
Hardy mums.
The word.

Took a chance,
showered during the thunderstorm, had to.
Made it quick.
As fern thorns snagged an opening drape.

#

Makeshift cover for the grill. And the narrative?
Fresh autumn leaves on the ground. Not splashing colour. As does the rain.

Your iPhone is not the facilitator

for your chronically late behaviour.
Saviour slice.
Might make a nice snack.

I repeat, avoid cliché. Like the Black Death. Repeat avoidance. Plagued by
"likes." Re: peat: a void dances. Like textual dredging. Like expiation.

Beneath my skull, beneath my hair,
the crawling notion of a woolly bear, an idea, fuzzy, headed where?

Came across a large stickbug crawling across the trail.
"That's huge!" she said.
"That's nothing," he replied. "When the dinosaurs roamed the Earth, those
bugs were as big as redwoods."

Closing the tome at p. 128 out of 698, I thought: Too much of a stretch. The
dust jacket flap would no longer serve as a bookmark.

Is that the sun coming up? I'd know it anywhere. There's a stain on my
trousers. Olive oil, shape of a pear.

there would be aches, beaches, each... and morning sand swept from wooden steps

#

After I carefully removed a tick, I was told to keep it for identification. When I
presented it to the bank teller she said, "That doesn't look like you."

Do not forget spatiotemporal context.
Who shall arrive with a ratio, hemp for all, pawn-flexed?

Memoir: the ice in my glass of ice water melted, and the water overflowed.

another day drafts to a close, slumped posture, rhetoricizing pose—
we used to drink straight from the garden hose

shadow of a hawk passing
beneath the cry of a blue jay

The remodelers came out and gave me my "complimentary estimate". They told me how tasteful and discerning I was. They called me handsome, truly sophisticated. And then charged me $75.00.

"Attagirl," said the software hacker to his dog as she shat on a neighbour's lawn. He realized then that his proudest achievement in life was the great disappointment he had become to his parents. Arseholes. Look at those lawn decorations. Uncle Sam, a Madonna. Skunk.

#

2020: From the flattened toads of spring to the smashed black walnuts of autumn—I wondered, walking that old road, where had summer gone? Summer of earthly ruin, bludgeoned justice, pandemic denial, executive ego-stench, blinding white malignity, all grinding on into the future.

blue skies, blue skies, aftermath
of smoke's demise, to these most fortunate
eyes wise enough
to surmise more smoke on the rise

insomniachybrachiopodcastireofdawn

Deep red maple leaves, from a distance—now, standing beneath them in noon sunlight:
translucent, bright!

"The branch snapped by the storm does not always fall in the storm," he said, adding, "as the proverb says," knowing it was not a proverb as far as he knew. He was speaking aloud, to himself, walking in the wind, the trees creaking all around him. That, he knew.

crimson shock of leaves amid the green sway—a yellow butterfly zigzagging my way—my "dying republic" never lived, what the hey?

Sunrise is a collapsing bench, sunset is fine. Sunset lifts with a little wine, sunrise settles you into the daily rising stench.

Indecision's fizz is
decision's fuzz.

my cat on the kitchen counter, enjoying his perch—he likes fish

The kite refused to settle
like the cowlick blown off
my neighbour's head in the wind.
Iridescence spun static effluvia,
nonappearance netting
a contingency unrelated
yet still easy to sense.
Dad and I used to ride out to Sherwood Forest to see what was going on.

Expression later in life took on a different hue, sang in a whisper in a more
shadowy pew. Reticence, brought to a boil, burned down the sanctuary,
splintering the foil of renewal's aberrancy.

Memo from Management: We sincerely thank the surveyed workers who
helped with our strategic plan. You clearly said you wanted change. Please be
advised, you're canned.

early autumn snow on the pond—no turtles basking on logs—genius

Part of a large oak tree fell on me today: a leaf.

Aubade: I hear church bells chiming seven, but they don't start till eight.
Do I see love and grace now reigning? Nah, just more ringing hate.

Fortuitous that my clipped toenail arced straight into my garbage pail. One less
nail to find in the rug. One more wonder worth a shrug?

The moon eases on, descends through the pines, disappearing into the haze, into its own fading glow. When it sets out of view, as the dawn lights the autumn trees across the valley, I'll return to bed. And dream? More erasure?

Cloud cover being pulled over the city like a blanket, which makes me feel like a bedbug.

Processing the report's conclusion, he probed the bullet hole in his head.

Monastically composing monostichs, I found myself stereophonically in stitches.

Looks like I let the day get away from me. Without a chase.

Flames don't dance, they spasm and writhe. Supplicants tithe.

Disconsolate as dust... the dust we ultimately are.
We sneeze!

#

Thinking back on our picnic last summer in the lush, sprawling clover. Came home with ticks. Guess it was a ticknic.

The past is gone? More here and now?
Wuzzy, izzy, onward plough.

After so many years, I caught up over dinner with my imaginary friend from childhood. What a tiresome, deluded, Republican creep he has become.

You find a grey hair of yours on the table in the sunlit room. Maybe lift it to the light, reflect, let it fall, and look for its descending glint brighter than ash.

Why, the nascent murk of meter
double-parked like a jolt of motion
delusional and fleeced,
refrain after free rain,

wit's sufferance grazing home plate's equilibrium.
It's all in the light,
winter's, angling for spring.

I crushed my solemn aspersions in the fields,
sought rhubarb in the ditches of early summer.
Summa faux exegete, so much for my...
remember?
Holy aureoles, ownerless slow days,
last laps dwindling, primed as salty ever after.

When he became a professional wine steward, his mother said, "'Wine
steward!' Hell, you're just another stewed wino."

The snow melted and there was my garden glove. Flat and wet, so flat and wet.
The future pelted and down swooped a hardened dove. Bitterly beset, bitterly
beset.

Craven as gravy's snooze slipping aft porous affliction torque-shocked rigor
ratcheting patched pelican dives a-cartwheeling sinking in slumber's pounced
green citing oneness in all sincerity next?

#

Not a floater, not a wader. A splasher!—
that bird flapping away in the shallow river.

He poured himself a glass of water. Took a sip. Now what?

Blossoming magnolia,
you don't see
the daffodils nodding
beneath your boughs as disciples,
and neither do I.

Old-timey time, flash me a fresh new moment. Thanks again.

You are thinning out the books, paring down, part of the long downsizing, so many must go, no genre spared, but the bookmarks, from bookstores, festivals, the ticket stubs, keep the bookmarks, you may need one, you think, putting another cherished book back on the shelf.

Standing alone at
the open window,
he would whisper his
songs and poems to the world,
seeking to join the passing breeze.

Flypaper feel of memory's release.

Twice more down and back. Twice more up and back. Twice more down and up. Up and down. Down and down, there and back, there, here.

He walked into the kitchen and noticed his wife's freshly baked bread. "That's an impressive loaf," he said. "Takes one to know one," she replied.

#

moonlight's stepping stones scattered on the lake's surface at dusk, here, there—later, the wider path

Wingnut, wingnut, spinning, spinning.
Hermes's helmet? Oh, that old tin thing?

The squeaky dog gets the treat. Today, not the remaining marbled meat.

There's my pocket comb. Washed and dried. Went through the wash. I nearly cried. Not about the comb. About the world. Peace scarce, flags wildly unfurled.

He'd had enough, he thought, and probably enough had had it with him.

Long, long, short, long whistle—
the train crosses the road.

Midnight lightning, early morning thunder—
the turtle ignores the toad.

orange crests, blue troughs stripe the lake's surface—mist clearing, turning to lace—
words scratching their way to cloudy

a must-see: the dust on the rust

country cemetery—
among the chipped and worn gravestones:
bright pinwheels planted,
spinning in the September sun

forever obfuscating restive
eternity's verisimilitude ever reaching

Release what's bound to disappear? Soul's thin clasp? The end of fear?

Demiurgic bumbling—
elephantine thunder rumbling—
if you see a storm stumbling your way,
hope it only tousles your hair.

"Still Your Mind" said the sign outside the yoga studio. Yes, I thought wearily,
it is still my mind.

hovering airy, solitary, and oh so visionary—the singing forth out o'er the sea...
  above the
blooming algae

III

Open up, said the season. In exchange for the word, I was sent on manoeuvres with a love letter from Michigan in my pocket. After the great quarrel, abiding, wincing at the figure "damaged goods", I penned a poem, an aubade of sorts. What could be done against it all?

Sunday overslept. Meanwhile legend after legend frayed like all the great love poems do, mid-August every year as we put off unpacking, thunderheads thirty miles east. Poems fizzled, frizzled then fizzled. Random gales delivered more origins to the sodden brain. "Indian Summer"?

Golly, hear that report? That's not dialogue. You and your bear claw were such a sight. So much a live poem, and who needs to write it down, just take it in. Sure I get bored. What's up tonight? We could start earlier to avoid the question.

"Vinny, Vinny, Vinny," I said, "no solution will redevelop lost spring trees in early leaf or my old Olivetti." It's like a hometown layover, a snapshot too brief to consider going home, coming back. A holiday beckoned, the glint of momentum missing from my morning inventory.

Poems, some aphorisms, Venice—the lists can be endless. If you regard tourists as fantasizing emperor moths, you may gain some insight into the landfill of "civilization". Lakeshore love song, glacial teardrop, help move us along to rest down by the river of sapience.

Again we were foiled, which prompted me to say, losing all patience, "I ask you, is that your banana on the counter or is it the intersection of Hope and Wisdom, a lost zone demanding lidless ignorance?"

Bourn

I

Towels only. In the bin. Think of the whole as you disintegrate in your hammock, listening for the gar's song. Where's that option sheet? Famous? How so? Focus. Frying like your brain in the public domain. Can we call the sky turquoise? Late arrival after late arrival.

You imagine moving toward the owl's call. Evening's leavening shade. Only nexus? Only a learned yawn?

Torpor heightens, a sustained yank of yield, an old take on the whole mess of time's innards creasing.

Dispersal lingers—actually its smoke—over an obvious improvidence. Blustery nothingness totters. Empty grind of ruin to rot, atomized—today's distractions scatter the remains of what, the latest exodus?

More havoc rustles free of the trunks in the attic, minutiae mocked on cue. Your overfilled kettles of ideals spill forth.

Or was it just a gravelly dream and a dead sway toward the rewrite of sanity's overwrought narrative deep in the headland ground down?

To opine pickled as a tier of odorless nonesuch, to fail to scatter the hail's expiring exchange: the toss that does not fade.

Ceaseless as fog in dreams only—a jab at the initial melody rallies dissonance, extending a oneness, useless and salient.

Forgetfulness at high tide like frost on the leaf, curious as false unction, or just rolling forth from source to source.

Pleased as understatement's blatancies, lilac intransitives, curses dear to the onion's splayed melody: arcing inscape's nod.

Mind's truncated song, utensils idling in the jammed drawer as we rejoice, qualms aside, now to utter what overshadows, what ignites the lingering clutter of sincerity's exultations.

Lyric assurance and timely episodes astir, a revival of the rumpled inner view—and a vintage gone awry... O larking grape.

II

missives sweetened, ontology rusting in the peppered harping of ego's roost...

open to a restive platter of hooey, a day, mist shifting, emblematically ripe

riffing now, perception's handle falsely elevated, vastly rearguard, but what does the moon owe you?

pageantry's hindrance, earthenware's realized form: how many other layers rival your most straightforward posturing

hinges creak like an etched sense of the redo, a makeshift tall order, a faint rally on the palette

endleaves give pause as you relive the cover's maudlin feel... and the odour of remembrance in pages held fast

reversals barely mentioned, slide off, some too rare—perhaps what we have is an earlier shine taken to the arcane

... may the mire be sieved on par, the runic plunge hidden in folds of illusory heft blanching at eked-out ratiocination

III

spirited winnowing at dawn all faltering gloss... as the atonal reign of
prophecy's echo rings more decay

sung to the tune of...

sliding along the horizon, the bulbous cargo ship—
sodden wad of chew between gum and lip—
fishpond Sunday evening, unctuous Tuesday afternoon—
cry of the chaos mongers, cry of the loon—

life is meaningless?—snip, eep, pip,
butterfly on the woodpile tells me to get a grip—
could the sky be peeling to a more idyllic hue?
ruddy lake turning a stony blue

four caws of the crow woke me from nettled sleep—
dreams a-roiling the sizzling shallow deep—
exertion's surface charms: a heap of ballyhoo—
I'll doze until a gale renders free the morning dew

The prospects ooze? Salute the seasoning. What emanates now only sharpens
the shred. I'll wave to the onrush, keep to the nadir. Speck or spark. Care
assumes the onus, garish in noon light. Ate? Tanked circus of the eaten.

Inscrutable hulking sun. Moody, sound. A grating and sour singe—go thank
yourself. Even you. Sans retinue?

Run as you go, flow as we flow, shave the smile from your face. Regard the
chemical haze drifting into the empty bay. Wavelet rush of wing-weary
plunge. A dog's single bark at the singular lark. A sufficient hunch to tighten
the long-faced empirical flicker.

magnitude's haze, alloy of wisdom with its knotty graces, a soothing
bewilderment easing an answer's rosy dissolve

IV

mind at "rest", faulty and knowing—catching... world's words again and again
and gone again

It took the surroundings, infused, to render me serious enough to dwindle
further afield.

a mere pose among the roses—
opting to maintain instead
something clear
of the faint thunder

Should we take down the drape, the blank canvas rigged against the sun? Lay
off the nuts?

The lance crossing the highway hit the iceberg as you planned, you say? A
storehouse of "presto!"—you croaker, you.

Got rid of my ticking clock. Now there's a sharp dripping behind the wall.
Maybe it's Earth, ticking away. Blam?

They took in so astutely what he did so resolutely—the twisting of the paper
clip out of shape
and then back, as he lectured so assuredly.

raw mosaic of verisimilitude ermine reversal, sweep of the stirred sky,
eventual as the next moment here as not

jeepers even if so morning allows a fresh array of illusions to issue the shifting
reset, interior ordination of wild cards typical not in the way the rain says
nothing though you may hear much in the flow

stars, stars, stars, etc. as I walked past the apple tree just as two apples fell

river's sparkle hovering above the flow—yellowing leaf's sheen wavering
beneath the glow

"stirred sky"?... whisked expanse of the sky... the sky's whisked expanse—
possession's decision clouds thinking in a rouged orangish blueswished way

the fitful happenstance
    of forethought's broach

  the flickering gleam in the eye of the stubborn roach

bench-clearing brawl... a butterfly fluttering, seeking to alight
                on a sheer, windblown shawl

Hannibal's mandible
                notwithstanding
the triangle's best angle

peeves quenched in a mutual drive forward to enclosure

            maybe just closure

ire's rigid equations

  a dispiriting luminescence leaks through the blinds

walnuts slow to ripen—a late fall—
      though relative to spring's late bloom,
    not late at all—

still, human emissions setting us all adrift—
      what's in a season?
                deadly shifts

Said the critic: Must I endure your cheesy verse once more? So be it; I'll
resume the grating chore.

Stretched to tear aft and fore
forever yonder—
    tension's aphorisms salt the fancy.

Sense of thought's feeling, why, in the long sweep of the moment's yarn...

About that taste of yours for
love's afterburner? No
finnicky sense
of what the dying fire yields—

time and its embassies of asphodel free and clear as the
        highlands in faint memory yeuking.

Take your time.
Under the (s)will of renewal—
    key in the lock.
    Essentialism is but a
  yearning deep in the heart
of nothingness, you.
    Never mind, flashes the egret's wings—
  sunrise rescinding.

Notice how
  the opening flatters
the veil, energizes,
    prompts you to listen closely,
  to instil in the silence
  a sense of memory's turns and widening ebb.

Sentient drift—
    sands to answer to and no deal
  down, the depths may
      own your laughter at a loss,
    as it goes, remember.
      a few more words for now...

Yesterday, to no avail,
      the crew-stroke of happiness
     trolling its refrain
  as the obvious ret(r)ains
        its tantrums.

Retinue everlasting
  beneath the flex of invisible laughter
easing not these xeric times, these orbits
     that levy the observable turning away,
  grainy sidestep of yore.

Alkanet root—its likening dye,
     again a keening sunset answering the invisible net, no etude, no terminus,

tensile as the florid restart that is autumn's true making.

A remnant uttered,
  a sleepless angle of static,
an exit to the tenor of belief's looping urges,
    filmic form—
all this as the moon rises
  over the wide river, emerging
   from light's blue to hang awhile,
    just like the old days, you laugh,
    then doze in the sheen.

More the music in the felt adjacency, the attribute,
	than any claim to "being"—

what's all the "this" in the "that"?

	Here's what I do with ease: cast these ideas to the breeze.

sway of the boastful cortege—
	meticulous as all enmity
  placed on the novice—
		imminent nonentities gathering
	a style
	  of tattered chime and rust,
	the tried and the rueful,
		the aimless feel of intrigue
  needled and seeping

the feisty function
	of contradiction
  requires just the right gladstone—
		sere locomotion,
		nostalgia for the flawless confluence

Here I sit, reading lightly, lightly reading, doing a little light reading, in light
read as light—nothing heavy here. What did Goethe say? Oh so many things.
What does Saturn say? Not "Look, see my rings!"

the drained sea's intel
	has it that narrative
	thenceforth shall encase
	a retrograde fixation
  on error roasted off-kilter
		with the grand manifold
	eaten already torn
  erstwhile recursively plagued

instilled in the known offering,
something near, far—
it all takes its toll, the embers,
the rarities that flare and endure,
radiance opening
like a map of this long ebbing trance,
all pennants ragged and reeling in the gale

one more petal comes unstitched,
falls from the flowery
quilt—heirloom
of billowing surprise

Just think. Just think. Just think...
the path of contraries, gospel
of harsh confluence
swaying in the poplars

mantra's anchor—

briny cloud, now a nest

of trumpets—
riddles assaying

a universe

in jest
the answers collect,
kindling for the harried air,
mulled, mobbed—
another earful of rubbish?

jewelled arc off course,

the known pitch of the barren hill,
   air murky in the mealy effluence—
one grows eager to rhapsodize

two words, a twinned offsetting, a whine—orders whispered, form of morning
shadows—reduced diviner slips us a clue

Rotting pumpkins on the neighbour's front steps
   atop the hill, begging
      to be rolled down the long driveway.
   Ah, youth.

Do not hesitate to ask, engrossed though you may be in your collection of
feldspar. When you hear footsteps thudding down the stairs and spilling out into
the snow, look to the source: the shock wave of submicroscopic circus clowns
tossing the sun off course.

A herd moves, a mote seen from atop the anvil. This is your expansive
moment, your brioche, its sheen. The dimmer switch allows the contours of
fatigue to drone on and off, fading this way and that, making a mockery of
afflatus. Innovation, glop, puff.

crunching acorn caps underfoot—
   crunching snow—
 steps floating on fallen blossoms—
      meadow's grass between the toes

out for a walk—dictating to my scribe, the passing breeze

In the event the whirlwind's mingling pursuits
         come to rest like a star's heat…

you may settle

for a capturing of the trivial angle
    sung by the choir of decline.

V

I was shovelling the walk, feeling my mind speed and sway, when the fir tree's shadow paused, scraped back the other way.

O the passing staticky razz of thoughts... as your old nodding rattling melon rots

Onions netted—to be peeled in the grand continuation of dense nothingness. Grandma patched my jeans. Silly thinking the future held some visionary sight for sore eyes. Over a plate of sorry fries.

Send yourself a reminder to check your reminders—does it bind, does it bind thee, shoes too tight for the bunion ballooning—that's a stretch, more of your wretched bassooning.

The freight train curves through the foothills—your stately lakeshore cabin, your towering trees—impressive; in a storm you may be asking for it. Take a lively spin through the dying mall. It's winter, avoid the ice, the dimly lit fall.

Some say the dead people in your dreams are spirits visiting you—I say, spare me... impossible.

all decked out idling forth avidly at leisure inseparable deeds in mind
fluorescently familiar as the pummelling vision tentatively offered
carnivalesque unleashed down to the bone discarded now held tight felt less
so now that was art

pelicans circle   hover
              swoop
                    dive
              in
                    wind
                    and rain—

          swirling rustle of the indistinct

O the many moods
Of remote mezzanine lighting—
  A grudging fragrance
  Takes you back

More clouds to hurry the darkness—more
Z's more mess

Remind me
to squeak
a single note more often

dusk, deepening blue of sea and sky—bright Venus dangling beneath tiny
Jupiter—shut up

VI

And so now not even that. I'll play quietly; we're all sleeping.
Curve it on the off chance the merriment goes boredom-free.
Your harried air shirks not only you but the reality bubble all round.

In stilled, remaining to delve: the outward manifestation, snow globe of
detachment. Spiralling through the smog, a crescendo of lucid song fails to
shear the gale to silence. Easy ire nestles, squirms, seeps into your tilled
illusions, low-strung and leonine.

ice in the grooves,
    a saintly glow to the oyster's dredged dreams,
room for more ooh and ah?

    bold as the hypotheticals bursting with juicy aplomb—
  fading pell-mell—
        the latest high-profile enclaves measuring wildly

gladness ephemeral as the
luminescence in the ant's eye—
  elation
  reflexive as a garden of puzzles—
oblige redraft
make a mockery of the plausible
    comeback bump—
  sort the uproar and shake out your pockets

More bombastic omnibus fumes
  immovable as the gilded anchor
 conspiring to sidetrack me
 from my
    own dim prophecies.
Sky-blue bay now in darkness—

dwell as you will? Do?
  Don't maim the martyred bouquet,
rubbish-wish—
  pinpoint, complicate,
best of luck with your flattening generalities.
Flopping back to life,
  the branzino leaps from my plate, splashes
  into the jumbo daiquiri
one table over—
  serves us all right.

Pile on the kindling
Light up more meaningless
Ice-cold filmic routine—

Swept away the sand between the ears—
  gibberish rubbed out to equate
  the rhapsodic proverb
  with cordially pulverized mud—

translucence fraught with environs—

repeat to what end
to peal ease
at length
this
a music a-bungle

Can't be serious you
  make jocular claims
  as the palm trees rattle
  north wind down from the plains—
  the mind and its directions—

Believe what you read

in the waves in that wind
  trudging the footprint-cratered beach
    wresting ideals, ah give it up?

The problem is the problem is the problem is a
succession of problems any minute now
any succession of nanoseconds
now your minutes
in it for no
other reason
under the sun's tincture of evasion

Salvation? Patient as lumber
  a mild idleness a
  lolling dilution—
  so finely overwrought
mercy seeps off and on
through the pores of the redolent pawn

More of the more
of the same as the frame
dissolves frantic as detonation
give me the placid oracle
more
jaunty mélange

Follow the foolish path
  to oblivion—
  foolish?
The only route
    swirling in the sporting sands of rhyme...
    recapitulate, exhale as you linger
    in the salvaged drop of gladness,
    in torn-porous heaven.

I was...

was was was—
daffodil blooming in the dune, dooming in the broom sweeping up fallen petals—
another hour raking up induced spoofery—

Forfeited, moot—
a quashing of the mercurial ciphering squeeze—
oath-rot, festival of indecisive parallels, deletion, fickle assembly surmised

seamless erasure as emergent thought—
    sidewinders far from idling through the void—
    destinations pooling, easing, formless

kaleidoscopic
  ever-resolving senses
          of understanding—

a crack in the traction
        a knock, a tabled break in the radiant action—

    shifting hue and sigh of the sea

... not to assess the slather in the name of gainsaying the map's reticular aims—
habit's numinous muddle

paramount in
the medley:

the revoked outlook
shabby and cleansed

coarse and roiled

teetering at the pinnacle:

premonitions meddling
with the lids
locks shorn
cleats buried in a seed coat's gleam:

all in a
raindrop's lit alette

VII

Broadened at low tide, the shore. "Another 'and' at hand and not an either/or."
Seeds from a pod cast astray.

Astray in the starry furrow. No more gifts, please, I'm downsizing in advance of
the next sneeze.

Another complex representation reduced. Currents ribboning in the sound. A
heady art expressly kinged.

    in the hush of hanging dust—

someone says, "continue"   someone asks "as what?"

bombardment's brassy laurels?

that kind of a world

to write it up, off

Burrowing under residue rising to meet the benevolent hum, I pause, wing it
again, instant by instant

as the sea shores up another gone day—and now to while away the dreaming
hours, you, once of the wildwood flowers.

A fine old time to gather your glum-glutton rhymes—and pitch them into the
scrolling itch, the meta slime.

Say something other than what you've said before. The proceeds shall
luxuriate. Not sure your spin cycle is working properly. The hay whispered:
mislay something else, something resting on your custom shelves. Selves.

beach holes holes on the beach holes in the sand what's down there?

Estimation thusly mundane and behind in the sequence, endlessly dealt,
empirically dished?

The foam sighs. Something eerie in the leaf; a dent in the placard surfaces a
knackered feeling. What spurs you on deters the yawn. Sleep's leaps peel back
the thin skin of the least of all worries.

Can the pill be crushed, the powder stirred into the sauce? Reiterate the slice
and rid yourself of the redo. Dust settles on the lip—you just can't feel it.

starry sky and beneath it all—resonant flesh mind and bone quieting to the
feel of moonlit stone

Once upon a time, many years ago,
There once was a once, twice bold I've been told
Thrice folded in lore, (legend's bullfice),
Quarce of a five-slice and a sixer on ice.

The wind blew in wild and woolly,
In from the west scourging, surly—
For two thousand days (or was it years?)
The ponderous opinions, the slathering jeers.

sun sending forth flares—
    how does your satellite fare?
  sanderlings scurry.

      doubtful exertion of the contraries
what do you propose
          more of the unarrayed day-spun sorely poised ore
odd taste the old knock of art at the door   a frosty creak

language   a fine word   for the grindy pathetic gunk to which it refers

106

O let go, let those tears fill your eyes... no mere call to moisturize

moon setting—handing off the glow of the dune to the sun

jam session: not sure who's playing what right now, right, what playing! who's sure... not... GOLLYWHAMIT!

Sour: dinner by Sysco, in every frickin' Frisco, and you there, sipping your settler pisco

corralled *oui, oui*... tossing back fistfuls of mess and inane melody—unity's numbing binge imbibing time's yearning slobber

look: a skink, doesn't stink (yet), it slinks, & blinks, I think

teetering offset for the energetic novice asking for garlic now in lock-ease larking slip

you asked for firm blubber, got a joshing waffler—down circled the crow sending the sunning turtles slipping into the pond—morning's gritty ideas, trailing gossamer

clearly... thinking's not... as sharp as before—prehistoric shark's teeth shift on the shore

fragments of music
        and resonance
    lingering

                elsewhere?

to frame a spreading storm
    in a second resown—
        counsel of the levelled grange—
    a slew of here

the icons give us
a flailing stare

    To let the verse
    speak to the curse
    of prosaic renown?

About the Author

David Wolf is the author of six collections of poetry, *Open Season*, *The Moment Forever*, *Sablier I*, *Sablier II*, *Visions* (with artist David Richmond), and *Weir* (a micro-chapbook from Origami Poems Project). His work has appeared in numerous literary magazines and journals, including *BlazeVOX*, *Cleaver Magazine*, *dadakuku*, *decomp*, *E·ratio*, *Exacting Clam*, *Indefinite Space*, *Lotus-eater Magazine*, *New York Quarterly*, *Otoliths*, *River Styx Magazine*, and *Transom*. He is a professor emeritus of English at Simpson College and serves as the poetry editor for *Janus Head: Journal of Interdisciplinary Studies in Literature, Continental Philosophy, Phenomenological Psychology, and the Arts*.

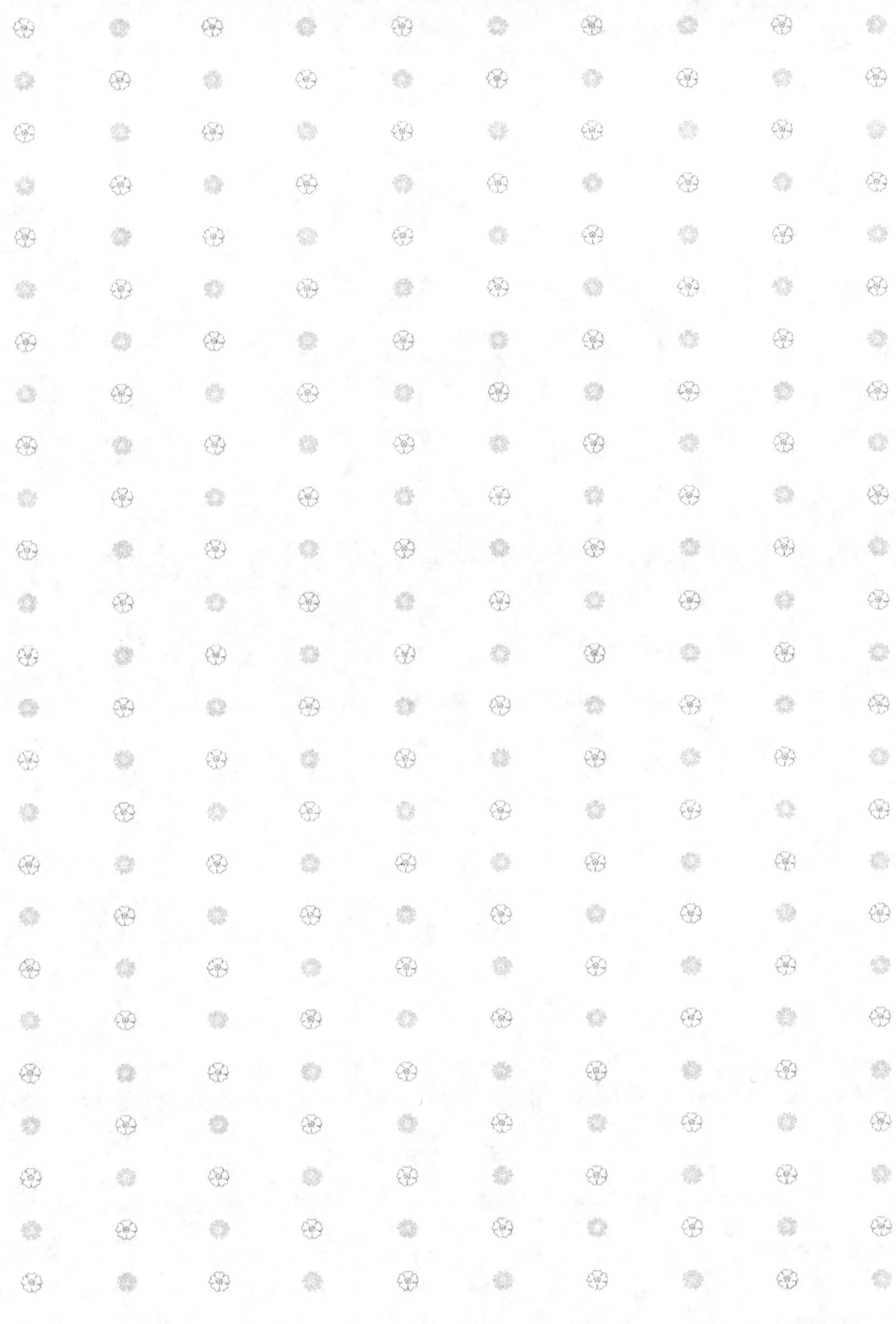

www.ingramcontent.com/pod-product-compliance
Lightning Source LLC
Chambersburg PA
CBHW082059090726
47909CB00011B/3084